Rethinking the Medical Brain Drain Narrative

Jonathan Crush

SAMP MIGRATION POLICY SERIES NO. 81

Series Editor: Prof. Jonathan Crush

Southern African Migration Programme (SAMP)
2019

AUTHOR

Jonathan Crush is Professor at the Balsillie School of International Affairs, Waterloo, Canada, and Extraordinary Professor at the University of the Western Cape, Cape Town, South Africa.

© Southern African Migration Programme (SAMP) 2019

Published by the Southern African Migration Programme, International Migration Research Centre, Balsillie School of International Affairs, Waterloo, Ontario, Canada samponline.org

First published 2019

ISBN 978-1-920596-45-3

Cover photo by Gallo Images/Daily Sun/Lucky Morajane

Production by Bronwen Dachs Muller, Cape Town

Printed by Print on Demand, Cape Town

CONTENTS   PAGE

LIST OF TABLES

EXECUTIVE SUMMARY

Concerns about the negative impact of the "brain drain" of health professionals from Africa have led to a dominant narrative in which those who migrate are a permanent, and costly, loss to the country of origin and a permanent, and valuable, gain for the country of destination. This brain drain narrative has a powerful hold on the way in which the migration of doctors is conceptualized and measured and its impacts are understood. National and international policy responses are similarly premised on the notion that all forms of cross-border migration are advantageous to destination countries in the Global North and damaging to health outcomes in origin countries in the Global South. South Africa is often seen in the migration literature as an archetypal African medical "brain drain" story. The post-apartheid departure of graduates from South Africa's medical schools has even been labelled "brain flight" and "brain haemorrhage" and a "deepening crisis" for the country's health system. Although some have contested the idea of a brain drain in specialisms such as surgery, the country's brain drain narrative has proven remarkably durable and continues to frame policy responses to the South African health care system.

In the new world of transnationalism, a global skills market, and greatly increased mobility by health professionals, it is unlikely that the traditional permanent-exodus model of the brain drain narrative adequately captures all forms of migration by South African doctors. Recent surveys suggest that a significant minority of doctors have experience working outside the country. To understand this finding, it is important to situate the experience of South Africa's physicians in the context of the opportunities that exist within destination countries in the Global North and Gulf States for the *temporary* employment of doctors. Global data on the temporary migration of doctors is scarce but there is enough evidence to test the dominant narrative that all doctor migration is permanent and therefore, by definition, harmful.

This report first examines the temporary employment opportunities for South African doctors in countries such as the United Kingdom, Ireland, Canada, and Australia. These include residencies, fellowships, locums, and various temporary worker programs. A 2013 SAMP survey of out-of-country employment found that nearly half of the South African doctors who completed the survey had worked in at least one other country. Fifteen percent had worked in at least two other countries. Some had worked in three or more countries, with a maximum of seven countries. As many as 61% of those with work experience outside South Africa had been to the United Kingdom. Canada was second at 10%, followed by some European countries combined (including Germany, the Netherlands, and Belgium) at 9%, Ireland (9%), and Australia and New Zealand (both 6%). Around 5% had worked in newer destinations such as the United Arab Emirates and Saudi Arabia. Most doctors who go overseas to work do so temporarily and for a limited period. Some 80% had worked in their first overseas country of employment for three years or less. Their reasons included financial inducements (including paying off student debts) and a desire to gain further training and skills. The main reasons for return were that their overseas job was temporary, that they had a permanent job in South Africa, and that they preferred being in South Africa for family and lifestyle reasons.

Given that many South African doctors have emigrated permanently over the last three decades, it is important to know whether those who have experience working temporarily outside the country are more or less likely to leave permanently in the future. The final section of the report therefore compares the emigration intentions of migrants (those who have worked outside South Africa) and non-migrants (those who have not). Only 50% of the respondents who had worked in a foreign country said that return to South Africa was permanent, which suggests that continued temporary or permanent migration is a strong possibility for many. Migrant doctors have marginally higher satisfaction levels with South African working and living conditions than non-migrants. At the same time, their overall levels of dissatisfaction are very high. This translates into significant and greater emigration potential among migrants. For example, 46% of migrants said they have given a great deal of consideration to emigration, compared with only 36% of non-migrants. Migrants also indicated that there was a greater likelihood of leaving than non-migrants. One-third of migrants and 26% of non-migrants said the likelihood of leaving within two years was high. At the five-year mark, the percentages were 52% and 48% respectively.

The report draws two major conclusions: first, the dominant brain drain narrative overlooks the complex nature of South African physician migration and ignores the fact that a significant number of doctors have temporary employment experience outside the country. Second, it suggests that temporary employment overseas increases the chances of permanent emigration later. The brain drain narrative needs to be rethought but it cannot be jettisoned. All South African doctors, migrant and non-migrant, still display extremely high permanent emigration potential. To date, government has failed to produce solutions to this intractable problem. Indeed, whatever the merits of recent policy initiatives to make healthcare more accessible to the population, there are indications that they will exacerbate rather than mitigate the brain drain.

INTRODUCTION

A recent review of studies of health professional migration in a globalized context noted that "the opportunities of health workers to seek employment abroad has led to a complex migration pattern, characterized by a flow of health professionals from low-income to high-income countries."[1] As a result, recruiting doctors and nurses from a low or middle-income country to serve the demand in high-income countries "effectively creates a shortage in the country of origin, and hence contributes to worse health outcomes."[2] Like most of the literature they review, their premise is that health professional migration is a zero-sum game, i.e. those who migrate are a permanent, and costly, loss to the country of origin and a permanent, and valuable, gain for the country of destination. This brain drain narrative has a powerful hold on the way migration of doctors is conceptualized and measured and its impacts are understood. National and international policy responses are similarly premised on the notion that all forms of cross-border migration are advantageous to destination countries in the Global North and damaging to health outcomes in origin countries in the Global South.

An analysis of the financial cost of doctors emigrating from various African countries to Australia, Canada, the United States, and the United Kingdom concluded that the cost to Africa in lost investment in training amounted to USD2 billion.[3] The study was criticized by one researcher as "unscientific", "indefensible" and "profoundly flawed."[4] One of the many objections was the failure to discount the value of remittances and to "assume zero economic effects from African doctors' remittances."[5] In particular, African doctors in the United States and Canada supposedly remit at least double the cost of their education to their home countries. Whatever the relative merits of these opposing arguments, they share one thing in common: an assumption that migration of doctors from Africa is a one-way, permanent move and that calculation of costs and benefits should be based on a model of permanent settlement in countries of destination.

South Africa is often seen in the migration literature as an archetypal African medical brain drain story.[6] The post-apartheid departure of graduates from South Africa's medical schools has even been labelled "brain flight" and "brain haemorrhage" and a "deepening crisis" for the country's health system.[7] Although some have contested the idea of a brain drain in specialisms such as surgery,[8] the brain drain narrative has proven remarkably durable and continues to frame policy responses to the underperforming South African health care system. The narrative has several key elements. First, because data on emigration from South Africa is notoriously unreliable, the story begins with statistics collected by destination countries and collated by organizations such as the Organization for Economic Cooperation and Development (OECD). For example, OECD data suggests that there are more than 8,000 South African-trained doctors in OECD countries, with the majority in Canada, Australia, the United Kingdom, the United States, New Zealand, and Ireland.[9] Smaller numbers are recorded in countries such as Israel, Belgium, Switzerland, and Germany. South African doctors are supposedly actively recruited and eagerly received in many countries for the quality of their training and expertise.[10]

Second, the brain drain narrative is underpinned by attitudinal surveys of the emigration potential of practising and trainee physicians, as well as the retrospective views of those who have already emigrated.[11] SAMP's 2013 online survey of South African doctors, for example, found that 40% had given emigration a great deal of thought and only 15% had never thought about it.[12] In addition, 40% had given it more consideration in the previous five years, while only 18% had given it less. Some 29% said they were likely to emigrate within two years and 50% within five years, while 51% had registered or written licensing examinations with an overseas professional body. Similarly, a survey of over 800 final-year students at eight South African medical schools found that 55% planned to work abroad after graduation.[13] A more recent survey of 260 students at three South African medical schools found that three-quarters had given some or a great deal of consideration to leaving South Africa.[14] Despite holding strong opinions about the negative consequences of physician out-migration for South Africa, one-quarter said it was likely they would leave within two years of qualification and 58% that it was likely within five years. A 2011 survey of first and final-year health sciences students at three South African universities (Cape Town, KwaZulu-Natal, and Limpopo) found that just over half intended to work in another country.[15] Finally, a study of final-year medical students in six African countries found the highest levels of interest in emigration among South African students.[16] Whether high emigration potential translates into actual departure depends on a number of factors but in the narrative, a large number of doctors are primed to leave and the brain drain is bound to continue.

A third component of the brain drain narrative is that push rather than pull factors are driving the permanent exodus of doctors from the country. Attitudinal surveys all tell the same story that there is extreme dissatisfaction with workplace and living conditions in

South Africa, which explains both the very high levels of emigration potential and departure itself.[17] The 2013 SAMP survey, for example, found that 63% of doctors were dissatisfied with their remuneration, 82% with their fringe benefits, and 90% with the taxes they had to pay.[18] In the workplace, 71% were dissatisfied with their relationship with management, 58% with their workload, 54% with personal security, and 48% with workplace morale. As regards living conditions in the country, 92% were dissatisfied with the prospects for their children, over 90% were dissatisfied with their personal and family safety, and 80% were dissatisfied with the cost of living. A more recent survey of over 2,000 doctors by the Colleges of Medicine of South Africa (CMSA) reported that "the most significant reason given by doctors for why they would choose to emigrate was personal and family safety and security."[19] In June 2018, the Minister of Health tabled a National Health Insurance (NHI) Bill in Parliament that will precipitate major changes in the way in which both private and public healthcare are delivered in the country.[20] One survey of healthcare workers' attitudes towards the NHI found overwhelmingly negative and sceptical sentiments, with over 80% of the opinion that the NHI would cause more emigration and half saying it would lead them personally to leave.[21] Alarmist media speculation is that the brain drain will accelerate even further with its implementation.[22]

The fourth strand in the brain drain narrative is that past policy measures and retention strategies to mitigate the brain drain have been unsuccessful.[23] The adoption of the WHO Global Code of Practice on the International Recruitment of Health Personnel was meant to slow the brain drain but has had little obvious impact on the outflow of doctors from Africa, as the numbers continue to rise in major destinations such as the United States, the European Union, Canada, and Australia.[24] As a result, "the current suite of retention strategies are either failing and/or targeting the wrong factors."[25] And, far from slowing the brain drain, government policies towards the sector are seen as a major factor driving it.

The final aspect of the brain drain narrative is that South Africans who have emigrated are a disengaged diaspora. A study of the medical diaspora in Canada found that, despite the perpetuation of a South African cultural identity, South Africa itself was often seen as a racial dystopia.[26] The study found minimal interest in supporting development initiatives and relatively low levels and volumes of remitting. Also, surveys of South Africans in Canada and other countries have shown that South Africans have very little inclination to engage in classic forms of return migration.

In the new world of transnationalism, a global skills market, and greatly increased mobility by health professionals, it is inherently unlikely that the traditional, uni-directional, permanent settlement model of the brain drain narrative adequately captures all forms of migration by South African doctors. This report attempts to re-examine the narrative and the evidence for more complex forms of mobility. In order to do this, it is important to situate the experience of South Africa's physicians in the context of the opportunities that exist within destination countries for the temporary employment of doctors. The next section of the report therefore reviews the surprisingly limited literature on the temporary employment of migrant doctors in several countries. The ensuing sections turn to the South African case, beginning with a description of the methodology and data on which the report is based. The findings on temporary migration that emerge from the research are then discussed. The final section returns to the issue of the brain drain narrative by asking if there are differences in the emigration potential of South African doctors who have experience working outside the country and those who do not.

TEMPORARY MEDICAL MIGRATION

Global data on the temporary migration of doctors is virtually non-existent but it is certainly necessary to test the dominant narrative that all doctor migration is permanent and therefore, by definition, harmful. There are hints in various destination countries that the temporary migration of South African doctors is an important phenomenon that needs further study. For example, Ireland has become an increasingly important destination for departing South African doctors. Yet the World Health Organization (WHO) reports that only 20% of South African doctors registered in Ireland practice exclusively in that country, which raises the obvious question about where the other 80% might be. Ireland is certainly a stepping stone to other destinations and experiences its own brain drain, which probably explains some of this discrepancy.[27] One survey of foreign-trained doctors in Ireland found that 23% planned to return to their home country and 47% intended to migrate onwards.[28] There is, therefore, a strong possibility that the missing 80% are now back in South Africa, have moved on to other countries, or are practising in both Ireland and South Africa.

The OECD puts the total number of South African-trained doctors in the United Kingdom at fewer than 2,000, yet the General Medical Council has over 7,000 South African medical graduates registered to practise. This discrepancy implies that there are many more

South African doctors registered in the United Kingdom than are practising there on a full-time or ongoing basis. A recent report on doctor migration to Australia, another major South African destination, distinguishes between permanent and temporary health professionals (both doctors and nurses) who came to the country to work between 2005/6 and 2009/10.[29] The temporary pathway is highly attractive to governments and employers given the ability to prescribe foreign doctors' location as a visa condition and allowing them to work for up to four years at undersupplied sites. As Table 1 shows, temporary workers (primarily on a skilled-temporary-work visa) outnumbered permanent immigrants by 71% to 29%. Of the 34,870 temporary migrants, 44% (or 15,342) were doctors. A further 2,420 temporary visas were awarded in 2010/11: 1,190 for general medical practitioners and 1,230 for resident (house) medical officers. The majority of the permanent and temporary South African health professionals are probably doctors. In which case, 78% were temporary migrants and 22% were permanent immigrants. Some would undoubtedly use the temporary-work visa as a pathway to permanence but an unknown number could have returned to South Africa.

TABLE 1: Top Source Countries for Permanent and Temporary Health Professionals in Australia, 2005/2006 to 2009/2010

Top 10 permanent source countries		Top 10 temporary source countries	
Country	No.	Country	No.
United Kingdom	4,120	United Kingdom	9,350
India	1,510	India	6,420
Malaysia	1,300	Philippines	1,850
China	970	South Africa	1,770
Philippines	510	Malaysia	1,570
South Africa	500	Ireland	1,560
South Korea	480	China	1,380
Egypt	420	Zimbabwe	1,180
Singapore	390	Canada	950
Ireland	350	United States	830
Total all sources	13,880	Total all sources	34,870
Source: Hawthorne (2012)			

As regards another major destination country, Canada, Table 2 shows that between 2010 and 2017, 4,161 specialists and 2,709 general practitioners entered the country on temporary work permits under the country's Temporary Foreign Worker Program (TFWP). One study notes that, instead of immigrating to Canada, International Medical Graduates (IMGs) often start out by obtaining a temporary work permit.[30] The authors argue that because work permits can be acquired more quickly than permanent residency, they are often used as a bridge towards permanence. The assumption here is that IMGs are cutting the immigration queue by using temporary status to gain permanent residence. However, this may not be the motive for all, particularly those who genuinely want work experience in Canada before returning home.

At a very general level, only 9% of all temporary foreign workers who arrived in Canada between 1995 and 1999 became permanent residents within five years of receiving their first work permit.[31] The level increased to 13% for the 2000-2004 arrivals and 21% for the 2005-2009 arrivals. The rate of transition to permanent residence was only marginally higher for higher-skilled than lower-skilled temporary workers. This suggests that most skilled temporary workers do not or cannot transition to permanent residence. Canada's TFWP has certainly been used by a number of doctors and their Canadian employers in recent years, although this seems to have tailed off (Table 2). Unfortunately, the data does not show the rate of transition for particular countries of origin.

TABLE 2: Doctors Working Temporarily in Canada Under TFWP

Year	Specialist physicians	General practitioners and family physicians
2010	1,870	440
2011	516	461
2012	531	470
2013	415	384
2014	237	408
2015	207	265
2016	198	187
2017	187	94
Total	4,161	2,709

Source: https://open.canada.ca/data/en/dataset/c65d2014-ef25-4781-b9b2-e13a7293b72d

Most Canadian provinces also have provisions for IMGs to work temporarily without being fully licensed. Provisional licences allow IMGs to practise without passing medical council examinations and completing the requisite Canadian postgraduate medical training. These licences are given different names in different provinces: "public service", "restricted", "defined", "conditional", or "temporary." They are usually given to IMGs willing to work in under-serviced, often remote and rural, communities in positions that Canadian medical graduates will not take.[32] In some provinces, such as Newfoundland, there are more provisionally licensed than fully licensed doctors. An analysis in 2005 found that South Africa was the major source country for provisionally licensed IMGs in at least five provinces (Alberta, British Columbia, Manitoba, Newfoundland, and Saskatchewan).[33] Provisional licences were also issued to South African IMGs in Ontario and Prince Edward Island. While provisional licensing is certainly a step on the road to permanent immigration for those who can fulfil the terms and conditions for full licensing, many IMGs in Canada are not able to get residencies and fulfil the other criteria for licensing.[34] For others, provisional licensing is simply an opportunity to gain skills and experience prior to returning home.

Another aspect of temporary doctor migration is the movement of postgraduates to take up residencies and fellowships in other countries. Canadian teaching hospitals have around 2,000 so-called "visa trainees" in residencies and fellowships, for example. At least half are beneficiaries of the Saudi Postgraduate Medical Program, which has expanded dramatically in recent years as Canadian medical schools derive significant financial benefit from the arrangement.[35] A recent study of where visa trainees were working after completing their training found that 24% were in Canada two years later.[36] Saudi trainees are obliged to return home but others do so too. South Africa has no equivalent programs for its medical graduates, although agreements do exist with Cuba at the first-degree level,[37] and for medical graduates from the United Kingdom to get further training and experience in South Africa.[38]

Another opportunity for physicians wishing to work temporarily in countries in the Global North is the locum tenens route. A doctor in locum tenens is defined by the British National Health Service (NHS) as "one who is standing in for an absent doctor, or temporarily covering a vacancy, in an established post or position."[39] In general, the number of locum opportunities is rising in Europe and North America. Locum opportunities are available to both general practitioners (family doctors) and specialists. A recent study in the

United Kingdom found that the number of hospital doctors choosing to work as locums almost doubled between 2009 and 2015.[40] In 2017, there were over 43,000 locum doctors in the country (or 18% of the total in practice). As many as 28% of locum positions were held by doctors trained outside the United Kingdom and European Union.[41] Private recruiting companies have sprung up to connect physicians and other healthcare professionals with locum opportunities. UK-based Globe Locums, for example, recruits globally online for locum positions in the United Kingdom, Ireland, Australia, New Zealand, and the United Arab Emirates.[42] In Canada, one recruiter advertises Canadian locum opportunities internationally as follows:

> Most Canadian physicians have time off during the year, whether it be for annual leave or vacation, and a very common practice in Canada is to locum. If you are an International Medical Graduate (IMG), and would like increase your Medical experience in a Canadian environment this would be a financially and professionally rewarding route to take. You may even be considering a full time job in Canada, and locums would be a good path to pursue in order to gauge if Canada is somewhere you'd be comfortable in working. Whatever your specialty is, often times there is a demand. You may be a general surgeon, Internist, or Psychiatrist, it doesn't matter – the need is there.[43]

Accurate global data on locum migration is not available. As one doctor in the United Kingdom observed, "it is incredibly difficult to collect locum figures because we're a hidden tribe in medicine."[44] However, this is clearly a growing phenomenon that South African-trained physicians have taken advantage of.

METHODOLOGY

SAMP has conducted two large-scale online surveys of South African-trained physicians working in South Africa. These were done in partnership with MEDpages, which emailed invitations to complete the online survey to all health professionals, including doctors, on its extensive database. The survey was completed by 745 doctors in 2007 and 860 doctors in 2013. Because this was not a random sample but a self-selected group of respondents, the responses may not be representative of the profession as a whole. However, these were among the largest migration surveys of South African doctors in the country and provide valuable insights into the emigration intentions of the profession as well as the phenomenon of temporary migration.[45]

The 2007 survey made the unexpected finding that more than one-third (35%) of the respondents had worked outside South Africa. The figure was even higher in the 2013 survey, which suggests that temporary migration may be becoming more common. However, the 2017 CMSA survey found that 593 out of 2,229 physicians surveyed (or 28%) had experience working outside South Africa.[46] Whatever the precise number, all three surveys confirm that a significant minority of physicians in South Africa have experience working in other countries. As the authors of the CMSA survey conclude, "many SA doctors work internationally for a period and then return to contribute to our healthcare provision. From a policy perspective, we need to guard against the view that doctors who work overseas are permanently lost to SA health."[47]

The 2013 SAMP survey incorporated additional questions designed to probe further on the issue of temporary migration, including where they had worked and their reasons for returning to South Africa. The findings about the temporary migration behaviour of South African physicians were supplemented with answers to open-ended questions at the end of the online survey and key informant interviews with South African doctors in Canada and South Africa in 2017 and 2018. As well as recounting their own employment histories, the interviewees provided insights into the employment histories of other doctors within their personal and professional networks.

MOBILE MEDICAL MIGRANTS

Nearly half of the South African doctors who completed the 2013 survey had worked in at least one other country. Fifteen percent had worked in at least two other countries. Some volunteered that they had worked in three or more countries, with the maximum being seven. Table 3 shows the overwhelming importance of the United Kingdom as a site of previous employment outside Africa (with 61% having worked there either as their main or second place of employment). Canada was second at 10%, followed by some European countries combined (including Germany, the Netherlands, and Belgium) at 9%, Ireland (9%), and Australia and New Zealand (both 6%). Around 5% had worked in newer destinations such as the United Arab Emirates and Saudi Arabia.

TABLE 3: Other Countries of Employment of South African Doctors

	1st country no.	Total %	2nd country no.	Total %	Total no.	Total %
United Kingdom	231	53.8	29	7.0	260	60.8
Canada	35	8.5	8	1.9	43	10.4
Ireland	28	6.8	9	2.2	37	9.0
Australia	15	3.6	10	2.4	25	6.0
New Zealand	13	3.1	12	2.9	25	6.0
United States	12	2.9	9	2.2	21	5.1
Gulf states	11	2.7	8	1.9	19	4.6
Asia	6	1.4	6	1.4	12	2.8
Other Europe	25	6.0	14	3.4	39	9.4
Other Africa	33	8.0	15	3.6	48	11.6
Other	5	1.2	6	1.4	11	2.6
Total	414	100.0	126	29.1		

Most (nearly 90%) had worked in their first country for less than four years (Table 4). They therefore do not fit the classic profile of return migrants who have settled permanently in another country and then make a subsequent decision to go back to their country of origin. Those who had experience working in a second country had been there for even less time (64% for less than a year compared to 35% of first-country respondents). These findings suggest that most doctors who go overseas to work do so temporarily and for a limited period.

TABLE 4: Period Spent Working in Another Country

Period worked	1st country %	2nd country %
<1 year	35.3	63.6
1–3 years	46.7	24.6
4–9 years	15.6	10.3
>10 years	2.6	1.6
Total	100.00	100.0

The temporary nature of work outside the country is confirmed by responses to the question of why they returned to South Africa. The respondents were asked to rate the importance of various push and pull factors in terms of their reasons for returning and the responses are combined in Table 5. As many as 61% said they returned because their job was temporary in nature and 64% because they had a permanent position to go to in South Africa. Other factors rated as important in the decision included family who wanted to return (45%) and to be closer to family still in South Africa, environmental factors such as climate, and social life. Other non-economic, quality-of-life pull factors included a preferable lifestyle and familiar culture. A desire to use their skills to serve poor communities was cited by nearly half. In general, quality-of-life factors were rated more highly than work-related reasons such as remuneration, job satisfaction, benefits, and workload. Overall, then, pull factors were more important than push factors in the decision not to stay away.

TABLE 5: Main Reasons for Returning to South Africa (% important/very important)

Push factors in other countries	
Job was only temporary	61.2
Family wanted to return	44.8
Inhospitable climate	41.3
Poor social life	38.7
No job satisfaction	35.3
Poor prospects for professional advancement	27.1
No job security	22.5
Insufficient remuneration	18.2
Inadequate benefits	17.9
Patients too demanding	16.5
Workload too heavy	11.0
Pull factors in South Africa	
Lifestyle preferable	77.1
South African culture	73.9
Closer to family	69.9
Permanent job in South Africa	64.0
Better social life	60.4
Greater job satisfaction	51.8

South African landscape/climate	51.3
Use skills to serve underprivileged	49.0
Poor prospects for professional advancement	39.7
Better education for children	37.0
Better access to medical care	34.7
Cost of living lower	34.3
Better job security	33.5
Better remuneration	29.7
Paid off medical school debts	26.4
Better benefits	26.3
Patients less demanding	18.1
Lighter workload	12.5

Complementary in-depth insights come from the qualitative material collected in the survey responses:

> *I have worked in England just after my house doctor year for six months in order to make some money to travel. At the time we did not need much to be working there. Lately it is more difficult to just go over and work. The South African skills are very practically-orientated and we are hard workers. That is why we are in demand all over the world.*

> *I trained here and went abroad to earn an income that would allow me to continue to work in the public sector on my return without being saddled with a huge mortgage. What was supposed to be a two-year commitment abroad was extended as house prices sky-rocketed and then the lure of obtaining a British passport. There had never been an intention to permanently emigrate.*

> *I was very happy living and working in the UK. I returned simply because I had met my future husband on a visit back home. I got an "equivalent" post in SA to the one I'd left behind in the UK.*

> *I was on a contract for two years and, after extending my contract, I stayed for another nine months and returned home mainly to enrol my son at a South African school in the Western Cape.*

I am an obstetrician. My work experience was much better in Australia. My income was better. The cost of living was not high there. I returned for family reasons in 2006 and since my return I have not been able to find a job in the health sector of South Africa. When my children finish their studies, I will not think twice of leaving South Africa again – it is much easier to find jobs overseas than it is locally – especially for a female obstetrician.

I have lived and worked in the UK for eight years – the reason was so that my husband and I could get UK citizenship – we now hold dual citizenship. The reason for wanting this is for safety. We are both Indian and although we love our country we feel threatened by the political situation. I would love to spend the rest of my life in SA but if I feel my safety is compromised, I will leave.

What motivates South African doctors to work outside the country? A survey of nearly 900 final-year students at eight South African medical schools found that of the 55% who planned to work abroad after graduation, three-quarters wanted to do so on a temporary basis.[48] One motivation is to get training and qualifications in a medical specialization through residencies and fellowships. In most countries to which young South African doctors are attracted, obtaining residencies is difficult because most teaching-hospital positions are reserved for locally trained doctors or for sponsorship agreements with other countries. For example, in 2017-2018, only 14 of the over 2,000 "visa trainee" residencies and fellowships in Canada for foreign-trained doctors were occupied by South Africans.[49]

In the United Kingdom too, access to training programme posts for non-UK/EEA doctors is restricted under immigration regulations. However, South Africans with British connections are often able to obtain UK citizenship and avoid visa requirements. Obtaining a residency or fellowship in a medical specialism is much easier for this category of young doctors wishing to advance their careers. In the SAMP survey, a total of 53 doctors (or 10% of the total who had worked overseas), had their highest qualification from an institution in another country (primarily the United Kingdom).

Locums have traditionally been a popular route for newly-qualified South African graduates who want to work in Canada. Rural and small-town Saskatchewan and Alberta are major destinations. In these two provinces, South African physicians made up 18% and 8%

respectively of the total physician workforce in 2009.[50] These doctors tend, in turn, to pro-vide locum opportunities for other South African doctors within their personal and professional networks. Some use this as a route to permanent residence in Canada while others return to South Africa. However, locum migration is not confined to these two provinces. One South African anaesthetist, for example, had also done locums in the cities of Toronto and Vancouver. The reasons for locum migration given in the survey are generally financial, although some doctors have broader motivations:

> I have worked in the UK, Brunei, Oman, the Emirates and New Zealand doing locums over the years and building up a nest egg abroad.

> I have been overseas (UK) to locum a number of times, to supplement income and to be able to holiday abroad. I have never had any intention of emigrating. However, should the government start implementing Zimbabwe-style land invasions or confiscation of property, I would not hesitate to move.

> I have lived for almost my entire life in South Africa, but have worked for short periods overseas. At this stage of my life I would love to work and travel in a different country for the purpose of not only treating medical conditions but also to experience different cultures and to delve into the history of that country.

> When I work overseas, I still work in Ireland for 2 months every 18 months for money and a break.

During the course of the research, other kinds of temporary or short-term working arrangements emerged. One was a private practice of four South African GPs in a major South African city. They also have a practice in the United Kingdom and, over the course of a year, each spends three months working in London. Also, a South African doctor in Canada had acquired dual citizenship and spent six months of every year working pro bono in South Africa and six months at a walk-in clinic in Alberta.

Private facilities in the United Kingdom offer many opportunities for work placements. There are an estimated 550 private hospitals and between 500 and 600 private clinics offering a range of services in England.[51] Most are required to have a Resident Medical Officer (RMO) on site 24 hours a day to cover for cardiac arrests on behalf of consultants. The hospitals vary in size, medical complexity, and workload but a typical private hospital will only handle elective surgery. Only the larger hospitals have intensive care or intensive treatment units and most of the clinical workload is general ward work and managing post-operative complications. Cape Medical Services in Worcester, England, is run by a South African-trained doctor and organizes 6-12 month placements for South African doctors in the UK private health system.[52] Most of these are contract positions as RMOs in acute care facilities. The RMOs usually work 168-hour shifts, during which they are required to remain on the hospital site at all times. The RMOs cover emergencies and general ward work, and some hospitals require RMOs to assist in theatre. As well as GBP1,615 per week worked, the doctors receive free on-site accommodation, General Medical Council registration, and advanced training courses.

South Africa's largest private hospital providers – Netcare, Life, and Mediclinic – have expanded overseas over the last decade, especially to the United Kingdom and the Gulf.[53] Netcare, for example, owns 57 acute care hospitals in the United Kingdom with 2,788 registered beds and 188 operating theatres. In 2015, Mediclinic purchased a 29% share in Spire, one of the largest private healthcare service providers in the United Kingdom. While there is no data available on the hiring practices of these facilities, it is likely that they have opened up opportunities for South African doctors to work for the companies in other countries. Interestingly, a review of online staff pages at South African-owned hospitals in the United Arab Emirates found that most specialists did not come from South Africa but from Asian countries such as India. However, the SAMP survey did show that the United Arab Emirates and Saudi Arabia have become desirable destinations for some South African specialists.

Since the end of apartheid in 1994, increasing numbers of skilled South Africans, including doctors, have moved temporarily to the United Arab Emirates and Saudi Arabia to work. Their migration is motivated primarily by the opportunities for earning significantly more than in South Africa. A survey of skilled South Africans in the United Arab Emirates showed that few, if any, intended to remain there permanently.[54] They visit South Africa frequently and most expected to return after working in the United Arab Emirates for several years. Some intended to move on to other countries. The recent high-profile Karabus case – involving the airport transit arrest and subsequent trial in Abu Dhabi of retired South African paediatric oncologist, Cyril Karabus, on manslaughter charges for the death of a patient in his care in 2002 – may, of course, exercise a dampening effect on doctor migration to the Gulf.[55]

RETURN AND REMAIN?

The final question addressed in this report is whether South African doctors with international experience are more or less likely to emigrate permanently from South Africa than their colleagues without such experience. In other words, does the opportunity to work in other countries make these medical migrants more satisfied with living and working conditions at home? The baseline for comparison are the doctors who have never worked outside the country (non-migrants). The major SAMP finding was that there is not a great deal of difference in the attitudes and perceptions of the two groups and the differences that exist are not statistically significant.

First, with regard to perceptions of working conditions in South Africa, migrant doctors have higher satisfaction levels on 12 of the survey's 18 indicators, but the differences are very small (4% at most) and do not fit a discernible pattern that could be related to their experience abroad (Table 6). For example, the migrants are marginally happier with workplace morale, infrastructure, available resources, and their fringe benefits. The only indicator with a higher spread was income, where migrants are more satisfied (by 7%) than those who have never gone abroad, possibly because of the opportunities to supplement local salaries with income earned abroad. Migrants are slightly less likely to be satisfied with the prospects for professional advancement, which could be attributable to experience of other healthcare systems.

TABLE 6: Comparison of Satisfaction with Working Conditions (% satisfied/very satisfied)

	Migrants	Non-migrants	% Difference
Appropriateness of training	83	80	+3
Relationship with colleagues	82	84	-2
Ability to find desirable job	68	67	+1
Workplace infrastructure	63	59	+4
Job security	61	63	-2
Workplace resources to do job	61	57	+4
Workplace morale	55	51	+4
Personal security in the workplace	49	46	+3
Prospects for professional advancement	43	47	-4

Workload	44	42	+2
Level of income	42	35	+7
Further educational/career opportunities	38	37	+1
Risk of contracting Hepatitis B	29	27	+2
Risk of contracting HIV	28	27	+1
Relationship with management	29	30	-1
Risk of contracting multi-drug-resistant tuberculosis	23	23	0
Fringe benefits	20	16	+4

In general, migrants are more satisfied with living conditions in South Africa with higher scores than non-migrants on 9 out of 12 indicators. However, once again, the differences are small and not statistically significant (Table 7). On only one indicator – satisfaction with ability to obtain desirable housing – is there more than a 10% spread. This could be related to higher earnings while abroad facilitating access to higher priced housing in South Africa. Migrants are less enamoured with South African government policies towards the health sector than non-migrants but the levels of dissatisfaction do not vary significantly and are extremely low (less than 10% satisfied) among both groups (Table 8).

TABLE 7: Comparison of Satisfaction with Living Conditions (% satisfied/very satisfied)

	Migrants	Non-migrants	% Difference
Medical services for family/children	68	64	+4
Desirable housing	66	55	+11
Good school for children	50	49	+1
Affordable quality products	31	27	+4
Cost of living	21	18	+3
Level of fair taxation	11	10	+1
Customer service	10	7	+3
Personal safety	7	8	-1
Children's future in South Africa	7	10	-3
Family safety	6	7	-1
Quality upkeep of public amenities	3	1	+2
HIV and AIDS situation	3	5	+2

TABLE 8: Satisfaction with Government Policies (% satisfied/very satisfied)

	Migrants	Non-migrants	% Difference
Import of foreign health professionals	6	8	-2
Government policy towards health sector	4	7	-3
Affirmative action	4	7	-3
Government economic policies	4	4	0
Black Economic Empowerment (BEE)	4	7	-3
Levels of corruption	0.2	0.5	-0.3

Levels of satisfaction among migrants are low across a range of living and working measures. Less than half of the respondents were satisfied with 10 of the 17 workplace indicators and 10 of the 13 living conditions indicators. Does this mean that migrants are more likely to join the brain drain of permanent emigration than non-migrants? Only 50% of the respondents who had worked in a foreign country said that return to South Africa was permanent, which suggests that continued temporary or permanent migration is a strong possibility for many. Overall, the survey found that those with experience working in other countries had higher emigration potential. For example, 46% of migrants said they have given a great deal of consideration to emigration compared with only 36% of non-migrants. Migrants also indicated that there was a greater likelihood of leaving than non-migrants. At each of three different time periods (within six months, two years, and five years) the proportion of migrants likely to leave for good was slightly higher (Table 9).

TABLE 9: Likelihood of Permanent Emigration by Migration Status (% very likely)

	Migrants	Non-migrants	% Difference
In the next six months	12	9	+3
In the next two years	33	26	+7
In the next five years	52	48	+4

CONCLUSION

The concept of return migration is usually associated with individuals who have emigrated to and effectively settled in another country, and then have moved back to resettle in their "home" country.[56] This concept, as traditionally conceived, does not adequately capture the complexity of doctor mobilities in the modern world. While some South African physicians clearly fit the traditional picture, research shows that the return intentions of emigres are actually very low. What we are dealing with, then, is a more complex category of physicians who work abroad for varying lengths of time from their base in South Africa. Although they exhibit slightly more positive attitudes than non-migrants to working and living in South Africa, only half say they are committed to remaining.

The global phenomenon of temporary doctor migration complicates the conventional brain drain narrative, which sees all departure as permanent and all impacts of doctors leaving a country as negative. The hegemony of this narrative partly explains why so little attention has been paid to mobile physicians and why, as a result, there is so little concrete data and research on the subject. While this form of mobility is undoubtedly more common in other health professions, particularly nursing, the evidence presented in this report suggests that it exists among doctors too. Certainly, it is a phenomenon that requires much additional research, not just in South Africa but more broadly as well.

ENDNOTES

1   Aluttis et al. 2014.

2   Ibid.

3   Mills et al. 2011.

4   Clemens 2011a, 2011b.

5   Ibid

6   Bhargava and Docquier 2008; Joudrey and Robson 2010; Kaplan and Höppli 2017; Mlambo and Adetiba 2019; Oberoi and Lin 2006; Özden and Philips 2015.

7   Crush and Pendleton 2010; Labonté et al. 2012.

8   Hutch et al. 2017; Liu et al. 2015.

9   OECD.Stat 2016.

10 Rogerson and Crush 2008.

11 Arnold and Lewinsohn 2010; Joudrey and Robson 2010; Bezuidenhout et al. 2009; Crush et al. 2012.

12 Crush et al. 2014.

13 de Vries et al. 2010.

14 George and Reardon 2013.

15 Naidu et al. 2013.

16 Burch et al. 2011.

17 Crush and Pendleton, 2012; Crush et al, 2014; de Vries et al., 2010; George and Reardon, 2013; George et al., 2013; Pendleton et al., 2007.

18 Crush et al, 2014: 26-27.

19 Van der Spuy et al. 2017: 550.

20 Hofman et al. 2015; Naidoo, 2012; Rispel et al., 2018, Smith et al., 2018.

21 Welthagen 2018.

22 S. Breakfast, National Health Insurance Could See Mass Emigration of SA Doctors: The Proposed Bill Could Further Compound the Existing Skills Shortage. *The South African.* 26 June 2018; M. Charles, Private Doctors Vow to Quit SA Over National Health Insurance. *Cape Argus* 27 June 2018; Anon, A Worrying Number of Doctors Say They Will Consider Leaving South Africa if NHI is Implemented. *Business Tech* 21 August 2018; I. Vegter, National Health Insurance Will Be An Unmitigated Disaster *Daily Maverick* 27 August 2018; Anon, Massive Wave of Doctors Leaving South Africa Ahead of the NHI. *Business Tech* 11 August 2019; T. Head, NHI Fears: SA Could Face a Shortage of Doctors due to Controversial Bill. *Sunday Times* 11 August 2019; K. Brandt, SA's NHI Bill Not Properly Thought Through, Says Doctors' Forum. *Eyewitness News* 13 August 2019.

23 George and Rhodes 2012; Crush and Chikanda 2018.

24 Tankwachi et al. 2015.

25 Crush and Chikanda 2018: 354.

26 Crush 2011; Crush et al. 2012.

27 Bidwell et al. 2013.

28 Brugha et al. 2016.

29 Hawthorne 2012.

30 Campbell-Page et al. 2013.

31 Lu and Hou 2017.

32 Audas et al. 2005.

33 Ibid.

34 Mathews et al. 2017a; Neiterman et al. 2017.

35 Mathews and Bourgeault 2018.

36 Mathews et al. 2017b.

37 Hammett 2014.

38 Connor et al. 2014; Kong et al. 2015; Reardon et al. 2015.

39 National Health Service, Guidance on the Appointment and Employment of NHS Locum Doctors Employment. At: https://www.nhsemployers.org/your-workforce/recruit/employer-led-recruitment/guidance-on-the-appointment-and-employment-of-locum-doctors

40 Moberly 2016.

41 GMC 2018: 8.

42 https://www.globelocums.co.uk/about-us

43 http://www.physicianlocumscanada.com/

44 Quoted in Oxtoby 2016.

45 Crush et al. 2007, 2015.

46 Van der Spuy et al. 2017.

47 Ibid.

48 de Vries et al. 2010.

49 CAPER 2018.

50 Joudrey and Robson 2010.

51 Mossialos et al. 2015: 52.

52 http://www.capemed.com/about.html

53 Mortensen 2008.

54 Fourie 2008.

55 R. Davis, The Abu Dhabi Nightmare Continues for Dr Karabus. *Daily Maverick* 21 November 2012.

56 Azose and Raftery 2019.

REFERENCES

1. Aluttis, C., Bishaw, T. and Franks, M. (2014). The Workforce for Health in a Globalized Context: Global Shortages and International Migration. *Global Health Action* 7: 23611.

2. Arnold, P. (2011). *A Unique Migration: South African Doctors Fleeing to Australia* (Seattle: CreateSpace).

3. Arnold, P. and Lewinsohn, D. (2010). Motives for Migration of South African Doctors to Australia since 1948. *Medical Journal of Australia* 192: 288-290.

4. Azose, J. and Raftery, A. (2019). Estimation of Emigration, Return Migration, and Transit Migration Between All Pairs of Countries. *PNAS* 116: 116-122.

5. Audas, R., Ross, A. and Vardy, D. (2005). The Use of Provisionally Licensed International Medical Graduates in Canada. *Canadian Medical Association Journal* 173: 1315-1316.

6. Bezuidenhout, M., Joubert, G., Hiemstra, J. and Struwig, M. (2009). Reasons for Doctor Migration from South Africa. *South African Family Practice* 51: 211-215.

7. Bhargava, A. and Docquier, F. (2008). HIV Pandemic, Medical Brain Drain, and Economic Development in Sub-Saharan Africa. *World Bank Economic Review* 22: 345-366.

8. Bidwell, P., Humphries, N., Dicker, P., Thomas, S., Normand, C. and Brugha, R. (2013). The National and International Implications of a Decade of Doctor Migration in the Irish Context. *Health Policy* 110: 29-38.

9. Brugha, R., McAleese, S., Dicker, P., Tyrrell, E., Thomas, S., Normand, C. and Humphries, N. (2016). Passing Through: Reasons Why Migrant Doctors in Ireland Plan to Stay, Return Home or Migrate Onwards to New Destination Countries. *Human Resources for Health* 14: Article no. 35.

10. Burch, V., McKinley, D., van Wyk, J., Kiguli-Walube, S., Cameron, D., Cilliers, F. Longombe, A., Mkony, C., Okoromah, C., Otieno-Nyunya, B. and Morahan P. (2011). Career Intentions of Medical Students Trained in Six Sub-Saharan African Countries. *Education for Health* 24: 614.

11. Campbell-Page, R., Tepper, J., Klei, A., Hodges, B., Alsuwaidan, M., Bayoumy, D., Page, J. and Cole, D. (2013). Foreign-Trained Medical Professionals: Wanted or Not? A Case Study of Canada. *Journal of Global Health* 3: 020304.

12. CAPER (2018). Annual Census of Post-M.D. Trainees 2017-18. At: https://caper.ca/~assets/documents/2017-18-annual-census_en.pdf

13. Clemens, M. (2011). No, British Medical Journal, The Emigration of African Doctors Did Not Cost $2 Billion. At: https://www.cgdev.org/blog/no-british-medical-journal-emigration-african-doctors-did-not-cost-africa-2-billion

14. Clemens, M. (2011). The Financial Effects of High-Skill Emigration: Lessons from African Doctors Abroad. In S. Plaza and D. Ratha (Eds.), *Diaspora for Development in Africa* (Washington DC: World Bank), pp. 165-182.

15. Connor, K., Teasdale, E. and Boffard, K. (2014). Working in South Africa. *British Medical Journal* 348.

16. Crush, J. and Chikanda, A. (2018). Staunching the Flow: The Brain Drain and Health Professional Retention Strategies in South Africa. In M. Czaika (Ed.), *High-Skilled Migration: Drivers and Policies* (Oxford: Oxford University Press), pp. 337-359.

17. Crush, J. and Pendleton, W. (2010). Brain Flight: The Exodus of Health Professionals from South Africa. *International Journal of Migration, Health and Social Care* 6: 3-18.

18. Crush, J. and Pendleton, W. (2012). The Brain Drain Potential of Students in the African Health and Nonhealth Sectors. *International Journal of Population Research* Article ID 274305.

19. Crush, J., Chikanda, A. and Pendleton, W. (2012). The Disengagement of the South African Medical Diaspora in Canada. *Journal of Southern African Studies* 38: 927-949.

20. Crush, J., Chikanda, A., Bourgeault, I., Labonté, R. and Tomblin Murphy, G. (2014). *Brain Drain and Regain: The Migration Behaviour of South African Medical Professionals.* SAMP Migration Policy Series No. 65, Cape Town.

21. de Vries, E., Irlam, J., Couper, I. and Kornik, S. (2010). Career Plans of Final Year Medical Students in South Africa. *South African Medical Journal* 100: 227-228.

22. Fourie, A. (2006). Brain Drain and Brain Circulation: A Study of South Africans in the United Arab Emirates. MPhil Thesis, Stellenbosch University, Stellenbosch.

23. GMC (2018). What Our Data Tells Us About Locum Doctors. Working Paper No. 5, General Medical Council, Manchester.

24. George, G. and Reardon, C. (2013). Preparing for Export? Medical and Nursing Student Migration Intentions Post-Qualification in South Africa. *African Journal of Primary Health Care and Family Medicine* 5.

25. George, G., Atunja, M. and Gow, J. (2013). Migration of South African Health Workers: The Extent to Which Financial Considerations Influence Internal Flows and External Movements. *BMC Health Services Research* 13: 297.

26. Hammett, D. (2014). Physician Migration in the Global South between Cuba and South Africa. *International Migration* 52: 41-52.

27. Hawthorne, L. (2012). International Medical Migration: What is the Future for Australia? *MJA Open* 1(S3): 18-21.

28. Hofman, K., McGee, S., Chalkidou, K., Tantivess, S. and Culver, A. (2015). National Health Insurance in South Africa: Relevance of a National Priority-Setting Agency. *South African Medical Journal* 105: 739-740.

29. Hutch, A., Bekele, A., O'Flynn, E., Ndonga, A., Tierney, S., Fualal, J., Samkange, C. and Erzingatsian, K. (2015). The Brain Drain Myth: Retention of Specialist Surgical Graduates in East, Central and Southern Africa, 1974-2013. *World Journal of Surgery* 41: 3046-3053.

30. Joudrey, R. and Robson, K. (2010). Practising Medicine in Two Countries: South African Physicians in Canada. *Sociology of Health and Illness* 32: 528-544.

31. Kong, V., Odendaal, J., Sartorius, B. and Clarke, D. (2015). International Medical Graduates in South Africa and the Implications of Addressing the Current Surgical Workforce Shortage. *South African Journal of Surgery* 53(3/4).

32. Labonté, R., Sanders, D., Mathole, T., Crush, J., Chikanda, A., Dambisya, Y., Runnels, V., Packer, C., MacKenzie, A., Tomblin Murphy, G. and Bourgeault, I. (2015). Health Worker Migration from South Africa: Causes, Consequences and Policy Responses. *Human Resources for Health* 13: 92

33. Liu, M., Williams, J., Panieri, E. and Kahn, D. (2015). Migration of Surgeons ("Brain Drain"): The University of Cape Town Experience. *South African Journal of Surgery* 53: 20-22.

34. Lu, Y. and Hou, F. (2017). *Transition from Temporary Foreign Workers to Permanent Residents, 1990 to 2014* (Ottawa: Statistics Canada).

35. Kaplan, D. and Höppli, T. (2017). The South African Brain Drain: An Empirical Assessment. *Development Southern Africa* 34: 497-514.

36. Mathews, M., Kandar, R., Slade, S., Yi, Y., Beardall, S., and Bourgeault, I. (2017a). Examination Outcomes and Work Locations of International Medical Graduate Family Medicine Residents in Canada. *Canadian Family Physician* 63: 776-783.

37. Mathews, M., Kandar, R., Slade, S., Yi, Y., Beardall, S., Bourgeault, I. and Buske, L. (2017b). Credentialing and Retention of Visa Trainees in Post-Graduate Medical Education Programs in Canada. *Human Resources for Health* 15: 38.

38. Mathews, M. and Bourgeault, I. (2018). Saudi Visa Trainees Called Home from Canada in Diplomatic Dispute. *The Lancet* 20 August.

39. Mills, E., Kanters, S., Hagopian, A., Bansback, N., Nachega, J., Alberton, M., Au-Yeung, C., Mtambo, A., Bourgeault, I., Luboga, S., Hogg, R. and Ford, N. (2011). The Financial Cost of Doctors Emigrating from Sub-Saharan Africa: Human Capital Analysis. *British Medical Journal* 343: d7031.

40. Mlambo, V. and Adetiba, T. (2019). Brain Drain and South Africa's Socioeconomic Development: The Waves and Its Effects. *Journal of Public Affairs* https://doi.org/10.1002/pa.1942

41. Moberly, T. (2016). Number of Locums has Doubled since 2009. *British Medical Journal* 355: i6206.

42. Mortensen, J. (2008). Emerging Multinationalists: The South African Hospital Industry Overseas. Working Paper No. 2008/17, Danish Institute of International Studies, Copenhagen.

43. Mossialos, E., Wenzl, M., Osborn, R. and Sarnak, D. (2015). *International Profiles of Health Care Systems* (New York: Commonwealth Fund).

44. Naidoo, S. (2012). The South African National Health Insurance: A Revolution in Health-Care Delivery! *Journal of Public Health* 34: 149-150.

45. Naidu, C., Irlam, J. and Diab, P. (2013). Career and Practice Intentions of Health Science Students at Three South African Health Science Faculties. *African Journal of Health Professions Education* 5: 68-71.

46. Neiterman, E., Bourgeault, I. and Covell, C. (2017). What Do We Know and Not Know About the Professional Integration of International Medical Graduates (IMGs) in Canada? *Healthcare Policy* 12: 18-32.

47. Oberoi S. and Lin V. (2006). Brain Drain of Doctors from Southern Africa: Brain Gain for Australia. *Australian Health Review* 30: 25-33.

48. OECD.Stat (2016). Health Workforce Migration: Foreign-Trained Doctors by Country of Origin. At: https://stats.oecd.org/Index.aspx?DataSetCode=HEALTH_WFMI

49. Özden, C. and Philips, D. (2015). What Really is Brain Drain? Location of Birth, Education and Migration Dynamics of African Doctors. KNOMAD Working Paper No. 4, World Bank, Washington DC.

50. Oxtoby, K. (2016). The Rise of Locums. *British Medical Journal* 354: i4292.

51. Pendleton, W., Crush, J. and Lefko-Everett, K. (2007). *The Haemorrhage of Health Professionals from South Africa: Medical Opinions.* SAMP Migration Policy Series No. 47, Cape Town.

52. Reardon, C., George, G. and Enigbokam, O. (2015). The Benefits of Working Abroad for British General Practice Trainee Doctors: The London Deanery Out of Programme Experience in South Africa. *BMC Medical Education* 15:174.

53. Rispel, L., Blaauw, D., Ditlopo, P. and White, J. (2018). Human Resources for Health and Universal Health Coverage: Progress, Complexities and Contestations. *South African Health Review* 2018: 13-21.

54. Rogerson, C. and Crush, J. (2008). The Recruiting of South African Health Care Professionals. In J. Connell (Ed.), *The International Migration of Health Workers* (New York: Routledge), pp. 199-224.

55. Smith, A., Ranchod, S., Strugnell, D. and Wishnia, J. (2018). Human Resources for Health Planning and National Health Insurance: The Urgency and the Opportunity. *South African Health Review* 2018: 23-31.

56. Tankwachi, A., Vermund, S. and Perkins, D. (2015). Monitoring Sub-Saharan African Physician Migration and Recruitment Post-Adoption of the WHO Code of Practice: Temporal and Geographic Patterns in the United States. *PLoS One* 10: e0124734.

57. Van der Spuy, Z., Zabow, T. and Good, A. (2017). Money Isn't Everything: CMSA Doctor Survey Shows Some Noteworthy Results. *South African Medical Journal* 107: 550-551.

58. Welthagen, N. (2018). Healthcare Workers' Knowledge, Insight and Opinion of the Proposed National Health Insurance. Report of Solidarity Research Institute, Centurion.

59. WHO (nd). *A Dynamic Understanding of Health Worker Migration* (Geneva: WHO).

MIGRATION POLICY SERIES

21 *Cross-Border Raiding and Community Conflict in the Lesotho-South African Border Zone* (2001) ISBN 1-919798-16-1

22 *Immigration, Xenophobia and Human Rights in South Africa* (2001) ISBN 1-919798-30-7

23 *Gender and the Brain Drain from South Africa* (2001) ISBN 1-919798-35-8

24 *Spaces of Vulnerability: Migration and HIV/AIDS in South Africa* (2002) ISBN 1-919798-38-2

25 *Zimbabweans Who Move: Perspectives on International Migration in Zimbabwe* (2002) ISBN 1-919798-40-4

26 *The Border Within: The Future of the Lesotho-South African International Boundary* (2002) ISBN 1-919798-41-2

27 *Mobile Namibia: Migration Trends and Attitudes* (2002) ISBN 1-919798-44-7

28 *Changing Attitudes to Immigration and Refugee Policy in Botswana* (2003) ISBN 1-919798-47-1

29 *The New Brain Drain from Zimbabwe* (2003) ISBN 1-919798-48-X

30 *Regionalizing Xenophobia? Citizen Attitudes to Immigration and Refugee Policy in Southern Africa* (2004) ISBN 1-919798-53-6

31 *Migration, Sexuality and HIV/AIDS in Rural South Africa* (2004) ISBN 1-919798-63-3

32 *Swaziland Moves: Perceptions and Patterns of Modern Migration* (2004) ISBN 1-919798-67-6

33 *HIV/AIDS and Children's Migration in Southern Africa* (2004) ISBN 1-919798-70-6

34 *Medical Leave: The Exodus of Health Professionals from Zimbabwe* (2005) ISBN 1-919798-74-9

35 *Degrees of Uncertainty: Students and the Brain Drain in Southern Africa* (2005) ISBN 1-919798-84-6

36 *Restless Minds: South African Students and the Brain Drain* (2005) ISBN 1-919798-82-X

37 *Understanding Press Coverage of Cross-Border Migration in Southern Africa since 2000* (2005) ISBN 1-919798-91-9

38 *Northern Gateway: Cross-Border Migration Between Namibia and Angola* (2005) ISBN 1-919798-92-7

39 *Early Departures: The Emigration Potential of Zimbabwean Students* (2005) ISBN 1-919798-99-4

40 *Migration and Domestic Workers: Worlds of Work, Health and Mobility in Johannesburg* (2005) ISBN 1-920118-02-0

41 *The Quality of Migration Services Delivery in South Africa* (2005) ISBN 1-920118-03-9

42 *States of Vulnerability: The Future Brain Drain of Talent to South Africa* (2006) ISBN 1-920118-07-1

43 *Migration and Development in Mozambique: Poverty, Inequality and Survival* (2006) ISBN 1-920118-10-1

44 *Migration, Remittances and Development in Southern Africa* (2006) ISBN 1-920118-15-2

45 *Medical Recruiting: The Case of South African Health Care Professionals* (2007) ISBN 1-920118-47-0

46 *Voices From the Margins: Migrant Women's Experiences in Southern Africa* (2007) ISBN 1-920118-50-0

47 *The Haemorrhage of Health Professionals From South Africa: Medical Opinions* (2007) ISBN 978-1-920118-63-1

48 *The Quality of Immigration and Citizenship Services in Namibia* (2008) ISBN 978-1-920118-67-9

49 *Gender, Migration and Remittances in Southern Africa* (2008) ISBN 978-1-920118-70-9

50 *The Perfect Storm: The Realities of Xenophobia in Contemporary South Africa* (2008) ISBN 978-1-920118-71-6

51 *Migrant Remittances and Household Survival in Zimbabwe* (2009) ISBN 978-1-920118-92-1

52 *Migration, Remittances and 'Development' in Lesotho* (2010) ISBN 978-1-920409-26-5

53 *Migration-Induced HIV and AIDS in Rural Mozambique and Swaziland* (2011) ISBN 978-1-920409-49-4

54 *Medical Xenophobia: Zimbabwean Access to Health Services in South Africa* (2011) ISBN 978-1-920409-63-0

55 *The Engagement of the Zimbabwean Medical Diaspora* (2011) ISBN 978-1-920409-64-7

56 *Right to the Classroom: Educational Barriers for Zimbabweans in South Africa* (2011) ISBN 978-1-920409-68-5

57 *Patients Without Borders: Medical Tourism and Medical Migration in Southern Africa* (2012) ISBN 978-1-920409-74-6

58 *The Disengagement of the South African Medical Diaspora* (2012) ISBN 978-1-920596-00-2

59 *The Third Wave: Mixed Migration from Zimbabwe to South Africa* (2012) ISBN 978-1-920596-01-9

60 *Linking Migration, Food Security and Development* (2012) ISBN 978-1-920596-02-6

61 *Unfriendly Neighbours: Contemporary Migration from Zimbabwe to Botswana* (2012) ISBN 978-1-920596-16-3

62 *Heading North: The Zimbabwean Diaspora in Canada* (2012) ISBN 978-1-920596-03-3

63 *Dystopia and Disengagement: Diaspora Attitudes Towards South Africa* (2012) ISBN 978-1-920596-04-0

64 *Soft Targets: Xenophobia, Public Violence and Changing Attitudes to Migrants in South Africa after May 2008* (2013) ISBN 978-1-920596-05-7

65 *Brain Drain and Regain: Migration Behaviour of South African Medical Professionals* (2014) ISBN 978-1-920596-07-1

66 *Xenophobic Violence in South Africa: Denialism, Minimalism, Realism* (2014) ISBN 978-1-920596-08-8

67 *Migrant Entrepreneurship Collective Violence and Xenophobia in South Africa* (2014) ISBN 978-1-920596-09-5

68 *Informal Migrant Entrepreneurship and Inclusive Growth in South Africa, Zimbabwe and Mozambique* (2015) ISBN 978-1-920596-10-1

69 *Calibrating Informal Cross-Border Trade in Southern Africa* (2015) ISBN 978-1-920596-13-2

70 *International Migrants and Refugees in Cape Town's Informal Economy* (2016) ISBN 978-1-920596-15-6

71 *International Migrants in Johannesburg's Informal Economy* (2016) ISBN 978-1-920596-18-7

72 *Food Remittances: Migration and Food Security in Africa* (2016) ISBN 978-1-920596-19-4

73 *Informal Entrepreneurship and Cross-Border Trade in Maputo, Mozambique* (2016) ISBN 978-1-920596-20-0

74 *Informal Entrepreneurship and Cross-Border Trade between Zimbabwe and South Africa* (2017) ISBN 978-1-920596-29-3

75 *Competition or Co-operation? South African and Migrant Entrepreneurs in Johannesburg* (2017) ISBN 978-1-920596-30-9

76 *Refugee Entrepreneurial Economies in Urban South Africa* (2017) ISBN 978-1-920596-35-4

77 *Living With Xenophobia: Zimbabwean Informal Enterprise in South Africa* (2017) ISBN 978-1-920596-37-8

78 *Comparing Refugees and South Africans in the Urban Informal Sector* (2017) ISBN 978-1-920596-38-5

79 *Rendering South Africa Undesirable: A Critique of Refugee and Informal Sector Policy* (2017) ISBN 978-1-920596-40-8

80 *Problematizing the Foreign Shop: Justifications for Restricting the Migrant Spaza Sector in South Africa* (2018) ISBN 978-1-920596-43-9

www.ingramcontent.com/pod-product-compliance
Lightning Source LLC
Chambersburg PA
CBHW080135270326
41926CB00021B/4497